Self-Care Tips for Glowing Skin

A no-nonsense Guide

By Sarah Joy-Mobley PhD

Self-Care
Tips
for
Glowing
Skin

© Copyright 2025

Printed in The United States of America

Sarah Joy-Mobley
PO Box 721
Sellersville, PA 18960

"

great things in business are never done by one person they are done by a team of people

--Steve Jobs--

Acknowledgments

Thank you
The Naked Peach staff, partners, and management.
Past. Present. Future.

This book is dedicated to my Grandma, Joy Mercedes, who lived till 101, all healthy years. She is my biggest inspiration on how to live an incredible and healthy life!

Table of Contents

Introduction

There are a few questions that I get asked often and one of them is my ethnicity and the other is my age. I am half African American and half Caucasian. My father who passed away, James Mobley, was African American, and my mother is Caucasian. I would be what some would call mulatto or mixed. I consider myself African American and I am proud of that heritage. "You put 50% of salt in your food you are going to taste it!"

My father, James Mobley, was African American. It is hard to talk about my dad and say the words without tearing up. I wish he was still here. He was a proud Alpha Male who always stood up for himself. He was a business owner and became a minister in his retirement years. He always encouraged me to be strong and stand up for myself and to never allow anyone to bully me.

Many people are stunned that I am over 40 years old, thinking that I am in my 20s or 30s. I have to giggle at times to myself. I have been through so much in my life and to think that I have aged well is quite a beautiful ending point, for me to begin my best life!

I had a rough start in life and when I was a teenager I ended up in the foster care system and then homeless. Thank goodness I had a lot of fortitude and will, and a fighting spirit to match. I always knew my life was destined for so much more than the cards I was dealt as a child. As young as five years old, I dreamed that my life would have purpose and that I would succeed at something. I just had to finally at some point in my life have a shot to go for it.

I have always been naturally curious, inquisitive and loved learning. When I was younger I used to bake, sell candy, sew and I learned how to be an entrepreneur to earn extra money.

My Home Economics teacher in high school took a liking to me in high school when she found out that I was a homeless teen. She would let me make hair scrunchies to sell at school during class. She would also show me how to make clothes for myself, so I could save money. I learned that even though I was on welfare and had a very small sum of money to work with that much was possible. I learned to be very resourceful with my money and took advantage of everything in my environment to make it work. I learned skills from everyone around me. I would make and sell things. I would bargain shop at thrift stores. My mind was always focused on trying to thrive even with very little.

I always played sports as a girl, so I learned in life that you just have to work a little harder, study and practice some more to win the game. That is why I love the book, "Mindset" so much because it gives people evidence about the two mindsets people have. One mindset is a "growth" mindset and the other is a "fixed" mindset. It illustrates the point that if you have a fixed mindset when you experience setbacks you see it as a failure or a permanent place. Whereas with a growth mindset you see setbacks as growth opportunities. Failure to someone with a growth mindset is not learning, not growing, not stretching to your true potential.

I am someone who has had to overcome a lot of challenges and gone on to open four successful salons in Philadelphia over the past 12 years. We pay our salon employees the highest commissions in our industry, and we have created great success together as a team.

I believe that my desire to pay the highest commissions in our industry and create a supportive environment is why we are able to do so well. I grew up around old school salon owners who treated their employees like partners; and paid them great commissions. That is exactly what I wanted to create at our salon. A modern day salon with old-school salon principles and values.

My true moment of successful transformation was when I decided to enter my zone of genius. I was always naturally gifted with an athletic physique. I saw on social media all these beautiful women with athletically toned bodies competing in NPC bodybuilding shows.

NPC is short for National Physique Committee. This is the same bodybuilding circuit that Arnold Schwarzenegger came up in. The NPC will take you to the IFBB league, which will then take you to The Olympia Stage. The Olympia Stage is where Arnold won his famous seven titles as Mr. Olympia.

When I saw these bodies I said, "Wow!" These women's bodies look exactly like mine. I remember when I was younger and used to model professionally. The photographers would tell me not to tense or flex my muscles. I remember purposely not trying to lift anything heavy when I was modeling, so I would not put on any more muscle than I naturally had. I remember being in elementary school and the kids would tell me to make a muscle all the time, because I naturally had muscles and was very athletic. They used to be amazed by my muscular physique.

My heart almost jumped out of my chest when I saw those women! They were being celebrated for being muscular, strong and athletic. My eyes and my heart melted. I thought to myself, I am sure I can do that!

Well as fate would have it, I was out one night with some friends. We were having a good time as we always do, and ended up meeting a personal trainer that night. We found out that he trains people for show competitions and that was the beginning of my journey!

I immediately began training for my first show with my son Julian, who also inspired me to work out and had a crazy metabolism for his age at 16. We both signed up for an NPC Competition in North Jersey. It was The John Kemper Classic Show. I entered the Masters Division, which was the over 40 age group. After standing in line to register my son and myself, the famous Steve Weinberger signed me in and commented on the fact that he could not believe I had a 16-year-old son. I took the compliment graciously and had no idea who he was. I was too new to the scene to know the ins and outs of everyone. Steve Weinberger was married to Bev Francis who was in the famous movie Pumping Iron II: The Women. She is now retired but was a professional IFBB champion bodybuilder. She and her former husband Steve own a gym in Long Island, New York, Bev Francis Powerhouse Gym. Their gym puts on many of these NPC competitions. The two of them are icons in the bodybuilding scene and well-known among celebrities.

I ended up placing first in my division. I felt like I was dreaming. I felt like a fish to water. I did not know how to do the bikini poses like the other girls, however, my modeling experience served me well because I felt confident walking and had stage presence. That was a beautiful moment for me. I learned some valuable life skills at the gym. If you put in the work, you will get results. The work you put in will reflect in the things and experiences you have. I also learned that there is no gain without some pain and no next level without sacrifices and giving up something. The meal prep for those shows is something else. You end up eating a lot of meals, however those meals are devoid of fats, carbs and sugar. You feel like you are starving and eating, all at the same time. It can be quite maddening the closer you get to competition day and the lower your carb-fat content is getting.

What I really like about the gym is that it is a fair environment. Always growing up I felt as if I didn't have an even playing ground to succeed. I would watch all my friends' parents pay for their college, buy them a car, pay for their weddings, help them put a down payment on a house, etc. etc. etc.

In the gym you cannot pay someone to get a six pack, you cannot inherit the six pack, you can't cheat for a six pack, you can't lie to get a six pack, you can't manipulate someone to get a six pack, you can't suck a rich dick for a six pack. If you want a six pack, you have to work out and diet really hard to get it. Disclaimer: If you are dating another body builder then they can help you with your abs, if you know what I mean!

At the gym the results clearly speak for themselves, and you can clearly see who is putting in the work. I personally like environments where to win, you have to put in honest hard work. I do not like to be in an environment where someone has achieved results without putting in their own hard work and effort. Then they try and make you feel like crap because you did not inherit the family fortune or compromise your values.

The other valuable lesson I learned at the gym was how to diet to keep muscle and lose fat, to become stage-ready. To end up on stage you have to use the Carb Cycle Diet. This is the diet all bodybuilders use to step on stage. You are eating a lot of high protein and limiting your carbs and fat intakes. You are basically cycling your fats and carbs to trick your body into losing the fat and keeping the muscle. I only recommend doing a carb cycling diet with a certified personal trainer who is used to training people for competitions. This diet can be dangerous for someone who is not experienced.

The spiritual lessons I learned from competing in a body-building show were, patience and gratitude. I had to plan out every meal and eat at certain times. I have never felt so grateful to have a piece of dry fish with nothing on it in my life. I learned that anything worth having takes time and effort. I learned the power of discipline by working long-term towards a goal and sticking with it by having persistence.

The craziest experience was after the competition was over and I had dieted for all those months to get ready for the stage. I remember having a piece of cake after the show and it felt like a train hit the back of my head. The flavors were like an explosion of sensations hitting my whole entire body. The sweetness was so strong that it felt like the whole cake was sugar.

That experience was my springboard into feeling like a winner for once in my life. Also, to be able to feel like my unique physique fit into a beauty standard that was celebrated and admired. "You got to get in where you fit in!"

Which leads me to want to say that all women are beautiful. Everyone on this planet has gifts, ideas, beauty, uniqueness and qualities that they need to share with the world. All living beings are made in the image and likeness of God. We are all one and equals in the eyes of God. God has put inside of everyone something valuable and unique and it's up to you to unearth it and bring it out into the world. Life is spiritual and we are spiritual beings having a human experience. As long as you are living and breathing, believe that God has put a purpose over your life.

All women are beautiful. Women are magnetic energetically. All you have to do is keep that energy flow open, free and flowing. People will be magnetized to you like bees to honey no matter your age, weight, skin tone, height or ethnicity. Men fall in love with our energy, our happiness, our vibe! Our essence as a women is beauty energy, sexiness, and prowess. Standards of beauty the media tries to push is an attempt to make women have low self-esteem to buy their products, services and watch their shows. King Charles loved and still loves an older women, Camella who was not the "typical beauty standard" according to popular media like his wife Princess Diana was. The fact of the matter is that the essence of being female is a pure magnetic vibrational energy that is ageless and timeless, and that is our essence. Men just love to suck that energy in like oxygen. Like Jennifer Lopez says, "Beauty is ageless and has no expiration date."

Winning the competition for me had my confidence on a high. I truly felt like I could do anything. That is when the idea started to brew for opening up a salon. I had been working as a freelance make-up artist for close to 15 years at this point. I had worked with salons, brides, clubs, casinos, celebrities, and models. The list of who, what and where could go on and on. Let's just say I was really good, really, really good and sought after. I did make-up for a few of Sean Combs' parties, Marcia Ambrosia, Christina Milian and many more.

I wanted to be able to start building a brand and a business of my own. I had worked with so many celebrities and would watch as one job dried up and they had to search for a new one. Sometimes they would have dry financial spells or lose a gig. For some of them the behind the scenes of their lives can be quite maddening. Their lives in the media look so fantastic. Meanwhile, some of them do not have a steady cashflow and can't pay their mortgage. Life on the red carpet can seem fabulous but their financial stability can be rocky. I also experienced that as a freelance artist. I would go on these great highs and have amazing experiences, then sometimes the work would dry up. I craved having something sustainable and consistent. I did not want a feast-or-famine lifestyle, which seemed to be the life of so many entertainers and celebrities. Someone was providing them with a paycheck. I wanted to be that someone, a business owner.

I had always been fascinated by business owners and always watched any manager or business owner carefully, especially if they were a women. I was always interested in what worked well for some businesses and what did not for others.

Anytime I had an opportunity to work for a business owner or manager I was always trying to look for ways that I could be of service or help in any way. I never understood those workers who tried to undermine the boss. I am still friends to this day with some of the managers and business owners I worked for. They are powerplayers in the business world and a great resource to call upon when needed. I learned early on to always add power to power.

Because of my innate desire to become a business owner one day, I decided to go back to school online for Business. I also went back for my Esthetician, Advanced Esthetician and an Esthetician Teacher's license. I was thirsty for knowledge because most of my life had been filled with just trying to survive. I read every book I could get my hands on and my mind started to expand while my world grew the more knowledge I acquired.

After doing a lot of industry research I decided to semi-retire from my make-up career and launch into becoming a salon owner. I wanted to stay in my circle of competence and that was the field of Esthetics, which is all things skin. An Esthetician is a Skin-Care Specialist, specializing in waxing, lashes, body treatments, facials, and make-up. I decided that opening a waxing salon would be the best type of Esthetician Salon for me to open based on my personal knowledge base. I had considered opening a lash boutique; however I wasn't as excited about doing lashes as I was waxing and facials.

Opening the salon was the biggest adventure I have personally taken on in my life. We started out with one salon on South Street, and we have now grown to four salons in total. The college degree that I think I should have gotten was a degree in Psychology because those interpersonal skills are everything!

However, I have grown and adapted over the years into being a business operator. The hardest thing I had to do was stop working as a technician. As we grew it was very hard for me to do the tasks of paying bills, replying to clients, handling issues, payroll, etc. etc. I had to take a step back and work on my business instead of working in my business. Because I had the foresight to be able to take a step into running the salons, we have been able to grow, and I have had a chance to grow our team.

I would say running a business is like being in a pressure cooker. If you can't handle the heat stay out of the kitchen. This year's goal is to have a Dream Team and Dream Clients. After many years of running the salons, my peace and sanity require me to be more discerning and knowing when to walk away from situations that no longer serve me. Thus comes from me learning how to have healthy boundaries with people. I read the books "Co-dependent No More" by Melody Peele and "Boundary Boss" by Terri Cole. I realize that it's not my job to Fix, Save or Rescue anyone. I should not be doing for anyone what they can and should be doing for themselves. When you get to a position of power, it's amazing the amount of people who will try and push your boundaries for their own personal gain.

I feel like the last 12 years of my life has been God planting me in the soil, so that I can grow spiritually; and fortify my character. I have learned so much about myself by being a business owner. I have learned how to be diplomatic, patient and to control my emotions. I have learned a lot about human nature and how people respond to fear. I can say I finally have gotten to a point where I can say, "Ok God, I'm giving this to you." I don't know how many times I have prayed and found grace through the many storms no one knows anything about. One thing for sure is God and prayer are always a part of my business and life plans.

self care
the practice of
taking an active
role in protecting
one's own well
being and
happiness

1

What is self- care?

There is a lot of buzz around the word self-care these days. I would describe self-care as, "The active practice of accepting, caring for, and advocating for oneself." Renee Brown is a licensed Psychologist, author and researcher on vulnerability. She describes self-love as,

●

"Practicing self-love means learning how to trust ourselves, to treat ourselves with respect, and to be kind and affectionate to ourselves."

●

I would say that I can identify with both of those statements.

Did you know that the human brain has over 60,000 thoughts per day. That translates to about 6.5 thoughts per minute. Unpleasant thoughts have a lingering effect on your mood and state-of-mind. The human brain, thanks to evolution, has a negative bias as a survival mechanism. Depression and anxiety are linked to the number of unwanted thoughts you experience and the issues that go unaddressed. Ruminating is when you focus on a thought pattern loop without addressing or exploring solutions.

The self-care practice of consistently repeating affirmations and practicing meditation are proven to help fight off the emotional distress caused by intrusive and negative thinking.

There has been a new movement in the psychology realm, which is called Positive Psychology. This new realm is flourishing because it does not believe in pathologizing people with labels. In other words, starting off with the premise that something is wrong with you. Instead Positive Psychology focuses on the fact that you are already whole, and nothing is wrong with you; and bringing that focus on building your strengths instead of focusing on your weaknesses. Part of being a human being is to have a wide range of thoughts, feelings and emotions, we just have to not judge our thoughts. We are not our thoughts, when we judge our thoughts that's when the pain comes. Just let the thoughts come and go and declare, "I disagree with that thought." Choose a new thought, get moving or work on something.

We all have things we are good at and we all have things we are not good at. In school we are graded on things. The teachers most often focus on what you are doing badly instead of what you excel at. It's like the boy who struggles with reading but excels at woodshop and art. He excels so much that the woodshop teacher declares that he's like a Master Craftsman. The intricate pieces of furniture and abstract designs he makes are breathtaking. In real life you get to focus on what you are really good at. The people who make the most money in life are the specialists. A medical doctor who is a family practitioner makes probably $100,000 a year, whereas a neurosurgeon makes over $500,000 a year. The riches are in the niches. That is why so many people do not end up financially in good places because they are trying to be everything to everybody. Instead of playing to their strengths and going all in and studying one specific thing and being an expert.

It takes over 10,000 hours to become an expert in your field. Think about how many hours you are devoting to your trade, skill or profession. The reason people do not excel at their strengths starts with the school system by having children focus on weaknesses instead of strengths. It happens in the medical field by focusing on what's wrong instead of what's good. I believe in taking a holistic and positive viewpoint on life and doubling down on your strengths.

There are many things you can do to increase your positive mindset. One of them is by practicing affirmations. There have been many studies done focusing on the benefits of daily affirmations. There is MRI evidence showing that certain neural pathways are increased when people practice self- affirmation tasks. Affirmations have been shown to decrease health deteriorating stress, (Sherman et al., 2009; Critcher & Dunning, 2015) and effectively used in interventions that lead people to live healthier lives, (Cooke et al., 2014). They help us overcome perceived threatening situations, (Logel & Cohen, 2012), are linked to positive academic achievement (Layous et al., 2012), and lower stress and help with ruminating thoughts, (Koole et al., 1999; Wiesenfeld et al., 2001).

The goal of saying affirmations is to bridge the gap from a pessimistic-negative bias mind to crossing the threshold into being optimistic and having a positive outlook on life.

Affirmations can also help you with your self-esteem and self-worth as a human being. Tell yourself what you want to become and who you are. If not the world around you will tell you who you are and define your worth!

Saying affirmations is a way to practice self-love. Also, taking time every morning to breathe deeply and meditate. To take a moment to just breathe in deeply, hold your breath and breathe out and hold. The practice of breath-work in meditation helps to bring you in the moment and also helps with self-control. Many people live their lives unconsciously just going about their day reacting, instead of having clear goals for their life and responding to the world around them.

There has been proven data on the effects of meditation and being able to respond instead of reacting. One of the most impactful books I have ever read was, "Man's Search for Meaning" by Viktor Frankl. He was an Austrian licensed Psychiatrist and Psychotherapist who was sent to Auschwitz concentration camp. He spent a total of four years at various camps and his whole family died in the camps. By the grace of God he survived. He went on to get his PhD in Philosophy after the war and advocated for the use of the Socratic dialogue, which is a self-discovery discourse for clients to get in touch with their spiritual unconscious. One of my favorite quotes from him is,

●

"Between stimulus and response there is a space. In that space lies our power to choose our response. In our response lies our growth and our freedom."

●

So, based on this psychiatrist and modern-day Positive Psychology, if you want true emotional freedom, it lies in your daily practice of meditation and affirmations. This allows your "monkey brain" as the Buddhist call it, to relax and go offline, so that your pre-frontal cerebral cortex can do the thinking for you!

Prayer is an activity that will help you strengthen your beliefs and spiritual practice. Having a spiritual practice is what helps you with your life's purpose and finding meaning in life. Believing in something higher and above you, having a daily spiritual practice like a gratitude journal, practicing acceptance, communing with nature to experience awe and wonder, feeling at peace and living life with intention, experiencing empathy for others, deep connections with others, a creative practice, and wanting to make the world a better place, are all very helpful.

Having a spiritual life can help you to cope with feelings of depression and anxiety as is having a sense of support in a spiritual community group that can provide social support. Research has shown that spirituality or religion can help people cope with everyday stress and negative feelings. When you are contributing to your own well-being, rather than how you look or stand in the spiritual community, make a difference. Prayer and spirituality have been linked to better health, greater psychological well-being, less depression, less hypertension, less stress, and more positive feelings.

I would suggest finding a spiritual church or religion that resonates with you. I happen to be more spiritual and not religious, even though I was raised as a Christian. I personally fit in better in more positive environments that don't use fear, judgement and hell as a tool for me to "behave." I believe in being optimistic and to know that I am already whole, and nothing is "wrong" with me. I just need to focus on my positive attributes and collaborate with like-minded individuals with a moral compass who have complimentary attributes to mine. Complimentary relationships always work out the best for collaborating. Someone who has the skill sets you lack, and your strengths are what they need. It is a beautiful dance between humans, and you can each appreciate and need each other without the components of competition and separation.

Ways that you can use spirituality to experience better emotional well-being:

*Pay attention to how you are feeling and accept both the good and bad feelings as part of being human.

*Focus on others to help you to feel more empathy, as helping others is an important aspect of spirituality.

*Meditate-pray for 10-15 minutes using breath work to calm your nervous system and develop a creative practice.

*Practice gratitude by writing down 10 things you are grateful for each day. Also, write down things that bring you happiness and focus a part of your day to happiness.

*Be mindful, become aware of your thoughts and patterns, be less judgmental of yourself and others. Thoughts are not who you are, so let them come and go without judgement.

I personally have a Gratitude Journal and a Self-Love Journal that I use every day as my spiritual practice. I have enjoyed them so much that I give them away for free at our salons. It has been wonderful watching our salon clients use them and greatly benefit from them as well.

One of the things that it says in the gratitude journal is that I have to say something nice to someone else, buy something for someone else or give something away. It is a constant reminder throughout my day to get out of my head and get in the present moment to try and help someone else. I will tell you that the beautiful moments of my soul have been from helping others. You just see their hearts light up with pure joy and it does feel so good. The best part about it is that every time I think about those moments those pleasant feelings come back. It is like a gift that always keeps on giving emotionally and spiritually.

It's funny how it seems so counterintuitive to help and give to others when maybe you might not have the things you need or be where you want to be. However, I can guarantee that the Law of Abundance states that you must give first for you to receive. Also, sometimes it might not even be your season to prosper. It might be a time that God is planting you in the ground so that your spirit and character can grow, so that when it is your season you can handle your success and be a good steward of everything that God has graced your life with.

Opening the salons put me on my spiritual path really quickly. I did not realize how stressful running salons would be with over 24 employees. I find that so many people who want to start a business focus on the "how" of having a business. To be successful as a business owner you have to focus on the "who." The person who has a strong will, is disciplined, has humility, can suffer, has a clear goal/vision, and can control their emotions can pull off just about anything. When pressures mount, do you get started or do you fold?

1. I would say that the main thing I notice as to why people don't succeed in life is they constantly start and stop their journey. It takes 10,000 hours to become an expert in any field. The only way to get to mastery is to take a journey and not stop. You have to develop a "come hell or high water" mindset.

2. Most people only do things when they "feel like it." This is why most people do not get much done. What could happen to your life if you decided you were going to do something and stick to it?

3. I would say that the main reason why most people can't is because they lack discipline, will power, and boundaries.

4. Having healthy boundaries is the best start to reclaiming your time and energy. Also, knowing what is and what is

not healthy in a relationship. When you reclaim your time, then you can reclaim your life. Sometimes that can even mean removing yourself from situations that no longer serve your greatest good. I have personally found that working out at the gym and training for bodybuilding shows was how I was able to strengthen those muscles.

There are a few books that I think should be required reading for all individuals in school, which are "Co-dependent No More" and "Boundary Boss." These books all cover the topics of what is healthy and what is not healthy in your relationships. I have found that it is up to you as an adult to do the painstaking work of rebuilding your life from the ground up. You can start by reading books to gather some basic knowledge and understanding. You can further seek out a therapist or a spiritual counselor to have some further insight into the tools you need to succeed.

Many coaches and therapists will work really hard with you to unearth your limiting beliefs, by learning what the root causes are of your triggers and negative thought patterns. They will help you to find positive emotional memories that are proof of the opposite, and to visualize these positive memories with emotion, as a way to reprogram those negative beliefs.

There has been a lot of research done on repetition and emotional engagement. A meta-analysis in Psychological Bulletin (Huang et. al., 2014) found that repeated exposure to positive affirmations combined with emotional intensity significantly increases the likelihood of changing underlying beliefs, as emotional arousal helps encode new information into the subconscious. Also, research indicates that during alpha (8-13 Hz) and theta (4-7 Hz) brain states, typically achieved during meditation or deep relaxation, there is increased neuroplasticity and receptivity to suggestion.

A study in Psychological Science (Lutz et. al., 2008) shows that these states enhance the brain's ability to rewire and adopt new patterns of thought. Developing and dedicating a 21-day self-care ritual to reprogram your limiting beliefs is a wonderful way to offer yourself self-love and compassion while forming a deeper, more secure relationship with yourself.

You will find that overcoming great odds and having to deal with trials and tribulations are a great asset in life. Dr. Martin Seligman, who has authored several books on Positive Psychology, studied over 1700 people who experienced the worst things that can happen in this life. Some of those things were torture, death of a child, rape, deadly illness, and jail. To Seligman's surprise individuals who experienced one terrible event had more intense strength and well-being than individuals who had experienced none. Individuals who had two terrible events were stronger than the individuals who had one. Also, the ones that had experienced three terrible events were stronger than the individuals that had two. Struggles build strength in the gym and in life!

I always had this theory of mine that my life's struggles had made me a stronger individual. However, it was interesting to see the data behind it. My biggest struggle in life has always been seeing people who have had life easy, who fall apart over things that I would find trivial. They get upset over things that I wouldn't even blink an eye at. I know how brutal life can be and I believe people need to work on fortifying themselves, so that they can bear down and get through life's trials and tribulations.

I feel like whatever life you have, you are either working to fortify that life and building it up, or you are busy in chaos and drama, tearing down your life. You are either part of the solution or you are part of the problem. That is why I love those books so much that I discussed them with you and even mentioned a few ideas that they conveyed. You will realize very quickly that it is not your job to fix, save or rescue anyone. Also, that is up to you to put the work in, read the book, go to therapy, save the money, eat healthy foods, and make good decisions for your own life. No one is coming to save you. It is you who has to do the work and save yourself. The flip side of not doing the work will be you ending up in your old age broke with no resources or education. You have to get out and get after it while you are young to build up a life you can enjoy in your later years when you do not have the mind, body or spirit and energy to remake your life. I always tell people to get out here and work on building up your life first. Enjoy life and relax later!

I have talked with so many older women in their 60s and 70s who have given up their whole lives to care for their families, children, older friends and other family members. They have been out of the workforce for so long that they do not even have enough work history to collect social security. Now in their older years they are working jobs at the grocery store and driving for Uber, etc.

I see this again and again, especially with women. We are often expected to be the caretakers and the ones to sacrifice for others. Well, if you work on yourself; you will learn real fast that not only is that unhealthy, you are also spiritually hurting yourself and others.

When you rob someone of their rock bottom, it doesn't help. Letting others have their own process to grow and learn is what helps. Their lesson sometimes comes during their darkest moments. So, that is where and when they will learn the lesson that most likely will turn their life around.

Many people live in fear and terror. They have not embraced accountability for their own lives and live in expectation and blame. They have a whole bag of tricks for why you need to be helping, saving and rescuing them. I suggest saying no, changing your phone number and sometimes you just have to move. You have to do whatever is necessary for your own peace and sanity.

You stop suffering by taking 100% accountability for your own life, because your life is 100% your responsibility. If you want to succeed or have contentment it's going to be up to you to make it happen.

That is why I am very Libertarian in my views because I believe in accountability and freedom of choice. Then, being responsible and accepting the consequences of that choice and that is where the lesson and growth happens to be for a sovereign individual.

The main thing that people struggle with is limiting beliefs and false narratives of themselves. Changing your beliefs can be very hard. You have created patterns in your life that are on autopilot and can be hard to reprogram.

I can try and explain my journey and what helped me to reprogram my beliefs. Your beliefs, self-esteem and self-worth are formed within the first seven years of life. Dr. Bruce Lipton author, scientist and PhD explores this theory in many of his books, specifically, "The Biology of Belief." He goes on to explain that between the years of zero to seven your brain is operating in the theta frequency, which is the lower vibrational frequencies that are open to forming your subconscious beliefs. You can achieve theta through meditation and hypnosis and then say affirmations as an effort to rewire this programming. I have found the best short cut to those efforts in the least amount of time is to go to bed listening to eight- hour videos from YouTube on the new beliefs you are trying to work on. I have listened to money affirmations this way, which worked the quickest on me.

I have such deep compassion for the people who grow up disadvantaged, homeless, or in foster care. People who did not receive the proper support and guidance at home as children are intrinsically at a disadvantage. Society is built upon a penal system and is not built to address environmental disadvantages. Many of the people who grow up in great homes go on to become a success very easily and effortlessly in life. Then when they see someone who does not fit their mold, they want to demonize them. That is why I am a huge proponent of people getting a vocational education to acquire a low cost career and just start reading as many books as possible. Go out and get the help you need from support groups and read books. Go to the library and check out books if you can't afford to buy them. Watch YouTube and learn as much as you can about health, nutrition, money, your skill set and mindset.

Where there is a will there is a way! Learning to love yourself and support yourself is the beginning of having purpose and meaning in your life.

self care is not
self
indulgence it
is self
preservation

--Audre Lorde--

29

2

Why Self-Care?

In order to live the life of your dreams and to look and feel beautiful it is important to practice Self-Love and Self- Care daily. It is sticking up for yourself and saying, "I matter." Your lack of preparation, chaos, last-minute nature and poor decision-making are not going to affect me today! I have boundaries and I am working on me. It is not my job to fix, save or rescue anyone. I have the power to say, "No!" Oprah Winfrey expressed in several interviews that saying "No" was the hardest thing she had to learn.

I like the quote from the famous philosopher Socrates,

●

"The Undisciplined life is an insane life."

●

Aristotle said it best as well,

●

"We are what we repeatedly do, excellence is not an act but a habit."

●

The ultimate form of self-love is discipline. Deciding what you would like to achieve long-term and setting into place daily, weekly, and monthly habits to achieve those goals through discipline. If you have carved out time for yourself to achieve your goals, passions and hobbies, then it is easier to say "no" to people when they try to encroach in on your time.

●

"Discipline is one of the highest, if not the highest, form of self-love. It is quite literally telling yourself that you will delay instant gratification and comfort for better things to come in the future. Discipline is trusting yourself by doing what you said you were going to do."

●

I like to make **"POWER HOUR"** blocks AM and PM to achieve my most pressing self-care habits that need to happen.

My **POWER HOUR** consists of:

❖ Waking up at the same time every morning

❖ Meditate and pray: 10 minutes

❖ Go over values and goals: 5 minutes

- ❖ Read something spiritual: 10 minutes
- ❖ Gratitude & Self-Love Journal: 10 minutes
- ❖ Shower: 10 minutes
- ❖ Skin-care routine: 5 minutes
- ❖ Dress: 5 minutes
- ❖ Vitamins and nutrition: 5 minutes

Self-Care **Power Blocks** consist of:

- ❖ Work out: 1 1/2 hours
- ❖ Read: 2 hours
- ❖ Research and study in my field: 1 hour

Self-Love **Nutrition Breaks**

- ❖ Breakfast (oatmeal and protein shake): 10 minutes
- ❖ Meal prep: 10 minutes
- ❖ Protein shake: 5 minutes
- ❖ Meal prep: 10 minutes
- ❖ Protein shake: 5 minutes

My nighttime **POWER HOUR** consists of:

- ❖ Gratitude Journal & Self-Love Journal: 10 minutes
- ❖ Writing down my to dos for the next day: 10 minutes
- ❖ Planning my next day's agenda: 10 minutes
- ❖ Prayer and meditation: 10 minutes
- ❖ Skin-care routine: 5 minutes
- ❖ Lay out next day's clothes: 5 minutes

- ❖   Pack next day's nutrition: 5 minutes
- ❖ Stretching: 5 minutes

Saturday is "Self-Care Saturdays." This is a day I get my nails, hair, massage and personal care done that I can't do for myself. This is also the day I will go out and have fun.

Sunday is for restoration and revitalization. This is a day for nurturing relationships only and getting out into nature. I also will go to church or church online. This is a day to restore. Also, to meal prep for the week. This way I hold myself accountable to my long-term personal goals. I want to live a healthy, vibrant, long and joyous life. Establishing a lifestyle of discipline gives you peace because you have benchmarks to hit. You feel accomplished after getting all of your self-care habits in. You gain trust and respect for yourself when you take care of yourself in a loving way and do not neglect yourself. Also, it is easier to say "no" to people when you have already decided how your day will be structured.

The rest of my time can flow. However, I have predetermined what I need for myself mentally, spiritually, emotionally, and physically. I love myself and respect myself enough to take time for me and not let anyone encroach on my ability to care for and love myself.

I find that my life goes much more smoothly when I create a schedule for myself that keeps me together. The more I care for myself the better I can show up in the world. When we neglect ourselves and live in chaos we are no good to ourselves or anyone else.

I have recently turned into a Self-Care Advocate because I understand the importance of people caring and advocating for their own well-being. I've noticed throughout my life that most of the chaos, confusion, and lack was purely self-imposed. I could also clearly see that people who were disciplined, had self-care routines, and self-control had amazing lives. This led me on my own journey to try and level up my own life. This would include going back to school, the gym, and reading books.

I was totally focused on what really works in life and how successful people became successful. I would say that it simply boils down to people's daily habits. Are your habits aligned with your long-term goals for success? You should ask yourself these very important questions. How can you learn the skills you need to level up your life? What type of environment can you surround yourself with to level up your life and be inspired?

The reason why so many people choose drama, gossip, drugs, alcohol, etc. is to distract themselves from the work they should be doing to level up and have a meaningful life.

fall in
love with
taking care
of yourself

3

Self-Care For Your Skin

I have spent the majority of my life in the skin-care industry. It all started when I was 14 years old, and the Mary Kay lady came to my house and showed me how to do my make-up and take care of my skin. I was hooked! I was already obsessed with the way my grandmother Joy lived a stress free and beautiful life. She gracefully took care of herself and her life with a series of rituals that made her life balanced and rich.

My grandmother lived to be 101 years old. Watching her live a life that was Artfully Created made me look at how I wanted to live my life. My grandmother woke up at the same time and did things like clockwork all day long. She was involved in several activities in church including the debate team. She would read, bird watch, play crossword puzzles, and simply enjoyed living based on her dedication to her disciplined life. I always felt safe around her because she was pleasant and even- tempered. I always knew what to expect from her because she had her life planned out.

She also ate healthy as well. All of her foods came from the farmers market, and she had a garden in the back yard. She would often make fresh sun tea that she would leave on the porch all day in the sun to brew. She would ask me to go out in the yard to pick fresh mint to put in the tea.

I miss so many of her rituals and habits that she did with so much love and care. She played the piano so lovely. My grandfather would light a fire in the fireplace and my grandma would serenade us with her music playing the piano.

She always taught me to think for myself. Gather all the information from reliable sources and then make a decision; also if new information comes along be willing to consider a new viewpoint. She was my hero growing up. A Captain in the Women's Army Corps and college educated. She was a small women with a big heart who lived a long life with much intention to living well.

The fact that my grandmother lived to such an old age, I always reflected on her life. I was always trying to figure out what was it about how she lived that gave her that longevity and quality of life. Health has always been something very important to me and something I try to cultivate on a daily basis.

Starting with one healthy habit is a surefire way to get on your way to self-care. I always try to get people to start with one healthy habit and from there build other healthy habits into a dedicated self-care routine.

When you are successful at one habit then you build confidence and trust in yourself and that success breeds more success.

I always start everyone off on a simple three-step skin-care routine AM and PM. You would be surprised how simply washing, toning and moisturizing your skin can make a dramatic difference on your skin. So many people go to bed with make-up on their face and then they have clogged pores that turn to acne and black heads. I have given facials on people who have not taken care of their skin, and it is like unclogging a drain sometimes.

Just like you have the habit of brushing your teeth, start taking care of your skin. Your skin is the largest organ on your body and protects you from environmental factors. Taking care of your skin in your younger years will have you looking 10 years younger than your contemporaries. Just look at J Lo. She is in her 50s and has had a heavy self-care routine since her early 20s. I'm not sure if I have personally seen anyone in their 50s that looks as amazing as she does. She has said that she stayed out of the sun in her 20s and 30s and that's what saved her skin.

I always suggest that everyone wear sunblock every day and reapply it every two to three hours for maximum effectiveness. Studies have shown that 80% of all aging comes from the sun. I'm not sure if anyone has seen the truck driver online that drove trucks for 30 years. One side of his face was in the sun and the other side was not; because of that his face on one side is soft and smooth and the other side is heavily wrinkled and aged. That photo is something worth googling, so you can see the severity of sun damage and its effects. Also, you can get sun cancer, sun spots and other problems associated with advanced aging.

The next step to fighting the ravaging effects of the sun is to make sure that you use an antioxidant underneath your sunscreen. My favorite one is L-Absorbic Acid (Vitamin C) because it has the most data behind it as being an effective antioxidant as well as brightening, anti-aging and keeping your skin clear.

Vitamin C is a favorite of dermatologists because it not only helps fight free radicals from damaging the cells of our skin, it also helps brighten the skin, control sebum production, which fights acne, and improves the appearance of wrinkles and fine lines. Vitamin C is such a powerful antioxidant that it helps treat and prevent photo aging.

Hydrate, hydrate, hydrate your skin!

Vitamin C is effective against both UVB and UVA sun exposure. Antioxidants work by neutralizing the free radicals that damage the cells due to UV exposure. At our salon, The Naked Peach, we have a Vitamin C Essence called Day Glow that has L-Absorbic Acid in it.

The Naked Peach's Day Glow Essence is a Vitamin C, amino acid and hyaluronic acid essence. This is a lightweight essence that can be easily added onto major parts of your body if necessary.

I know that if I am out in Las Vegas or Miami I will put Day Glow Essence on my whole entire body then sun block to make sure my skin is covered!

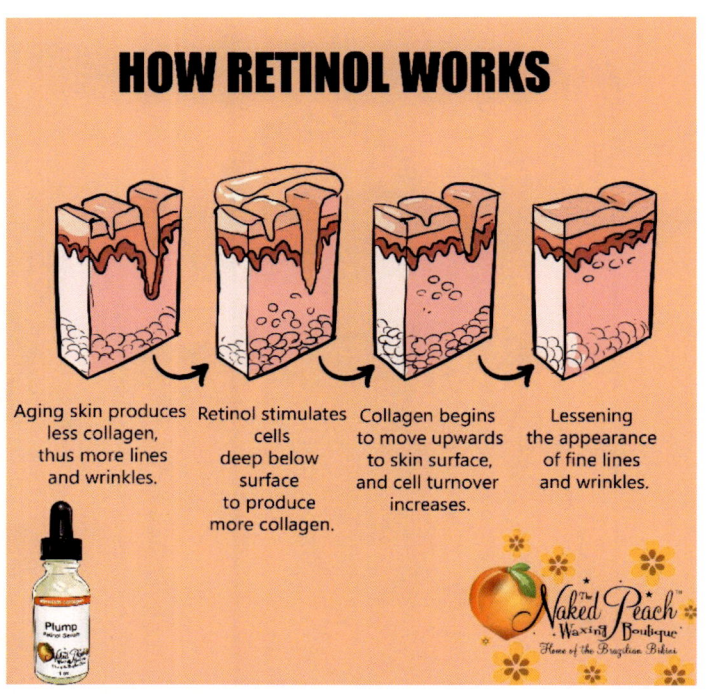

HOW RETINOL WORKS

Aging skin produces less collagen, thus more lines and wrinkles.

Retinol stimulates cells deep below surface to produce more collagen.

Collagen begins to move upwards to skin surface, and cell turnover increases.

Lessening the appearance of fine lines and wrinkles.

The gold standard for treating aging skin is Retinol. I will be talking about the over-the-counter usage of Retinol to keep it simple for the everyday consumer. Retinol is a form of Vitamin A and has been around since the 1970s. Retinoids are stronger, and they must be prescribed by a doctor. However, Retinols can be purchased over the counter and are in many skin-care products. I personally find prescription Retinoids very irritating to my skin, so I go for the over-the-counter versions. I find that I get the same results without the side effects of the prescription. I find that a lot of people find prescription based Retinoids intolerable, and many dermatologists recommend using an over-the-counter Retinol instead.

There are years and years of data showing that Retinol works to help the cells turn over faster, thus creating new cells. Retinols encourage the skin cells to divide more rapidly thus building up a protective top layer of the epidermis. Retinols also increase the production of hyaluronic acid, which keeps the skin moist and plump. Retinols also help to block inflammatory pathways that can lead to pimples and acne.

I always recommend that women over the age of 30 start incorporating Retinol into their skincare routine. I always encourage usage every three nights and to build up to every other night. It is best to use Retinol at night for the most effectiveness.

At The Naked Peach salon we have a Retinol serum called Plump. It is a lightweight serum made with other powerful peptides to add in the process of keeping your skin youthful and smooth.

Another hallmark of youthful skin is even-toned skin. Skin that is hyperpigmented and has sun spots on it looks more aged. I personally like the ingredient Alpha Arbutin to lighten and brighten my skin. I happen to suffer from hyperpigmentation on my face. I find that with the daily use of our products containing Alpha Arbutin I can keep the spots at bay and they disappear. However, with melasma and sun spots you do have to use a serum every day or they will come back. The issue with sun damage is that the damage is deeper in the skin and those dark damaged cells work their way up into the top layers of the epidermis over time.

Alpha Arbutin is a derivative of Hydroquinone. Hydroquinone, is a controversial ingredient to purchase over the counter. I now only recommend that clients use that ingredient under the supervision of a dermatologist because it can irritate the skin if over used or not used according to the skincare plan.

Alpha Arbutin is a natural alternative to hydroquinone, and it will help to reduce uneven skin tone and hyperpigmentation. This ingredient is mostly extracted from the bearberry plant, as well as made synthetically in the lab.

It works primarily by stopping melanin from concentrating in certain spots. It works on sun spots, acne marks, brown spots, freckles and more.

One of the best sellers at our salon is The Peach Bleach, which has Alpha Arbutin in it and also Yarrow Flowers, which helps with ingrown hairs. We also have a newer product dedicated for the face called Light & Tight. It has Alpha Arbutin in it to lighten-brighten and it also contains Acetyl Hexapeptide-8, which is a substrate of botulinum toxin and functions in the same way that Botox does to relax the muscles of the face.

Finally, in the ingredient category for anti-aging self-care steps to look more youthful are peptides. Peptides are short chains of amino acids that are naturally occurring and synthetically made. My personal favorites are Acetyl Hexapeptide-8, Palmitoyl Oligopeptide, and Palmitoyl Tetrapeptide-7. These peptides have been proven to produce collagen, firmness and elasticity in only a 12-week period through clinical trials.

You can find several products at The Naked Peach that contain these peptides. Plump, Porcelain Doll and Light & Tight are all packed with powerful anti-aging and collagen-building peptides.

Hyaluronic acid is another wonderful skincare product to be using in your anti-aging skincare arsenal. Hyaluronic acid is a naturally occurring part of your skin. Hyaluronic acid attracts moisture to your skin, making it appear more plump and youthful looking. At our salon we have Porcelain Doll serum. I always like to spray The Naked Peach's Thirst toner on my skin first and then apply Porcelain Doll to lock in all that good moisture. You want to use the serum while your skin is still damp to lock in the moisture and then follow up with a moisturizer to seal everything in.

I also like using an ultra-rich night cream to lock in all of the serums I apply to keep my skin hydrated overnight. I personally like using the Whipped Facial Butter from our salon The Naked Peach. Whipped is packed with peptides, marine collagen, squalene, hydrolyzed elastin and glycerin. This luxurious facial butter will keep your skin soft and supple while locking in your other serums.

When it comes to skin aging it's important to use a wash that is gentle and does not strip the skin. I personally like to do a double cleanse. One with a cleansing balm or oil and a second with a gentle cleanser. This ensures that all the make-up has been removed from my face, still feels hydrated and all of my natural oils have not been stripped away. At The Naked Peach Salon we have a Swept Away gentle cleanser and Melt Down Cleansing

Balm for a gentle double cleanse. They are part of my product empties on a regular basis. They keep my skin clean, clear and hydrated.

The KEYS to youthful looking skin have Five Pillars.

1. Even tone of skin

2. Hydrated skin

3. Smooth skin

4. Lines and wrinkles are not pronounced

5. Lower jowls have a lifted, full and tight appeal

self care

is how you

take your

power back

4

Skincare Facials for Youthful Skin

The rise in recent technology and social media has helped many women and men have access to knowledge that was previously limited to a few rich nobles and celebrities. There has been a push in our industry to live more healthy lives and to seek youthful appearances that are not so "plastic surgery looking."

I have personally found that eating healthy foods, working out, drinking water, taking supplements and a proper skincare routine are all the right ingredients to looking youthful and feeling youthful as well.

All of the above habits are things that are within your control. You have the power to work out, you have the power to eat healthy foods, you have the power to put on sunblock and take care of your skin.

Maintaining all these habits over time will make you look youthful, healthy and vibrant. When you do get into your 40s and 50s you will not look like a train wreck. You will have aged like a fine wine. You will just get better with time.

So far we have addressed the skincare products and ingredients that work for making the skin look more youthful. It is time to start discussing some of the facial machines that you can use at home or facial services you can get to enhance your results for a more youthful appeal. I will talk about what I personally use and find useful.

Red Light Therapy is a proven way to get added anti-aging benefits as well as to help with anxiety and depression.

If you were to shine a light through a prism it would fragment into all the colors that make up the visible spectrum of light, including green, blue, purple, yellow, orange and red. Most wavelengths of light do not penetrate the skin deeply at all and instead are absorbed by the surface layers of the skin. Unlike the other colors, red light easily penetrates the skin, which makes it useful for therapeutically reaching cells and tissues deep inside the body.

Unlike sun rays that cause a burning of the skin, red rays protect the body from damaging radiation and bolsters energy production inside every cell with which they interact.

Red Light Therapy has been researched and documented for over 100 years. However, it has been of special interest since the year 2000. There has been a huge interest in Red Light Therapy in the United States.

I personally recommend it to the women who cannot stop sunbathing and love a tan. When visiting salons that have Red Light Therapy booths, I tell them to stay in there for 30 minutes so they can get the feel, warmth and sensation of lying in the sun without the damaging effects. Then I tell them to get a spray tan and take an oral vitamin D tablet. The sun provides the much needed vitamin D, which helps with depression and anxiety. However, laying in the sun is not worth the damage done to the skin. The sun actually damages the DNA in the cells of the skin.

Some of the incredible benefits of Red Light Therapy are increased energy, helps to combat aging, makes the skin look healthier, reduced wrinkles and helps get rid of cellulite. It also improves mood and cognitive function.

My wakeup call to start staying out of the sun and looking for alternative ways to feel the benefits of the sun, was from doing makeup at weddings. I would see the bride, mother- of- the-bride, the grandma and the sister-in-law. I was always in shock to see the person who laid out in the sun every day for hours with no protection, just some oil. Their skin literally looked like a leather bag. I could not believe how it aged women. I would be doing makeup on a women in her 30s and they would look 60 with the sun damage. I was sold in those moments on the importance of sun block, staying out of the sun and having healthy alternatives for a tan.

When I give myself a facial I make sure to lay under the Red Light Therapy device I have for 20 minutes. I also put it over the top of my stomach because it has been shown to help with weight loss as well. You can use it several times a week.

Another tool I use to help with my facial tone is a **Micro-Current device**. There are many devices on the market. I prefer to use a Micro-Current device with EMS technology. That way I am stimulating different depths of muscle tissue on my face.

Working out in the gym my whole life and seeing the results of how my skin looks because I have good muscle tone led me to be a believer in the concept of Micro-Current. Your face has hundreds of muscles and it's the only part of your body where the muscles are attached to the skin. Micro-Current works by stimulating the muscles to retrain them. Thus in theory by working the muscles of your face your overall tone and appearance will look more lifted and youthful. Micro-Current increases the ATP in your skin, which is the main source of energy for cells to function properly. This cellular energy is necessary for the production of collagen and elastin in the skin.

Treatment suggestion: two-three times a week for 12 weeks and then continue once or twice a month to maintain.

Micro-needling is another great way to help promote collagen and elastin production by causing micro-injuries on the skin by penetrating the epidermis. Thus causing the cells to have to produce new collagen and elastin to repair the micro-injury; causing the epidermis to thicken and get firmer. In his book titled, "Dermal Needling," Dr. Lance Setterfield goes into extensive detail about the benefits of Micro-needling. He gives before and afters of clinical studies showing women who needled along their jowl lines and the results were astounding. They had a more lifted jaw line; lines and wrinkles were diminished, and their skin was smoother. This book really helped me to further understand the benefits of needling and also how this is a well-documented service that can bring significant results without invasive surgery.

Depending on how deep you go with the needling will depend on whether you will need some numbing cream. I can tolerate a cosmetic needling done by an esthetician and do not need to have the numbing cream. If you are going for a deeper medical-grade needling than I would suggest getting numbing cream. This service is especially good for women who have deep lines and wrinkles, sagging jowls, acne marks and large pores.

Treatment will vary depending on the client's needs and severity of issues. I would not have this treatment more than once a week if I am pushing for results. I'm a firm believer in giving your skin a chance to heal and recover. Just like working out at the gym. You never work on the same muscle every day. You work different body parts, so you have time to heal and recover.

Radio Frequency is another popular technology that is non-invasive. Radio Frequency works by creating heat within the skin and provides a quick tightening effect. Heat makes the collagen in the skin contract as well as helps with long term collagen production. It works to tighten lax skin on the jowls and neck, and it helps with wrinkles.

While lasers work on the surface of the skin, RF works by delivering wavelengths of energy safely to the deeper levels of the dermis, helping to improve the tone, structure, and even lifting the tissues.

There is peer-reviewed data backing up clinical trials to confirm that RF promotes changes in the tissue conformation, inducing neocollagenesis by thermal generation in deep layers of the skin tissue, thus being able to treat wrinkles and skin laxity. This process leads to a tissue repair response, establishing a long-term dermal remodeling.

This service feels like someone is taking a warm stone over your face. It is quite relaxing and feels good. Typically, I will do this for 20 minutes on each side of my face. I will only do this a maximum of one day a week for four-six sessions. Again, I like to give my skin a chance to rest and recover.

Dermaplaning is my favorite manual ways to remove dead skin from the surface of the skin. Not only does dermaplaning remove dead skin from the surface of the skin but it also removes vellus hairs (aka baby hairs) from the face. I find that I like to incorporate dermaplaning into my skincare routine after I have done a chemical peel and all the skin has basically peeled off of my face. That way any other dead skin that was left behind will be removed with the dermaplaning blade. This service is also a good step to add to a week of event facial. Removing all of the facial hair always allows the make-up to lay smoother on the skin, avoiding any type of shadows that might be cast from facial hair.

Dermaplaning uses a sterilized stainless steel scalpel that is meant for the lighter hairs of the face. I find dermaplaning to be more efficient than dermabrasion for the removal of dead skin.

Dermaplaning is great at removing dead skin and surface hair, it is also superb for allowing products to penetrate the skin deeper and further.

There are a lot of people who worry about the hair growing back thicker. I have been dermaplaning my skin for over five years and the hair grows back like the original baby hairs I removed.

Normally, this service calls for planing on skin dry. I have had great success dermaplaning with oil on the skin. I typically use our Relax oil, which is a sweet almond oil. This oil does not clog the pores or cause irritation. It is an anti-inflammatory oil and can be used on all skin types. I find that planing with an oil reduces the risk of nicking my skin or other people's skin in a facial. I find that it also gives smoother results.

Another beauty hack I use to achieve even, clear and younger skin are two types of peels. One is **TCA and the other is a Salicylic Acid Peel**. These two peels I find are the best at addressing a multitude of skin issues. Chemical peels exfoliate the skin without having to scrub the skin. This peeling process happens with the chemicals. TCA (Trichloroacetic Acid) is considered The gold standard in chemical peels. TCA is derived from acetic acid, a derivative of vinegar. TCA works by coagulating the protein in the skin and causing the skin to frost. This causes the skin to peel as well, helping to rid the face of dead skin, clear pores, even out skin discoloration and smooth the skin. When using this peel your skin will start to tighten over the next few days and then start to peel. The skin left underneath after your skin has shed off like a snake's skin, is baby smooth!

Salicylic Acid is another favorite of mine that helps the most with white heads, black heads, acne and clogged pores. It is a Beta Hydroxy acid, and it is able to penetrate into the pores and unclog them, basically degreasing them. Salicylic Acid is a naturally occurring compound, which can be isolated from the bark of the willow tree. It can also be synthetically produced as well. Salicylic Peels do not flake the skin like TCA does. I like to combine the two peels together for maximum effectiveness. I prefer to put on a layer of TCA 20% and Salicylic 20% together. I usually do this on a Monday, so my skin can peel during the week and by the weekend my skin is silky smooth like a baby's!

Out of all the skincare treatments I do. I feel as if the peels are the most important in overall general appearance of the skin in the shortest amount of time.

There has been so much controversy lately about all of the celebrities who are coming out with skincare lines. The controversy lies in the fact that they are really not telling their customers what they are really doing with their own skin, with their estheticians, dermatologists and plastic surgeons. Customers truly do want to look and have skin like many of these celebrities, however they need to be transparent in everything they do to achieve that look. There are some celebrities that do show what they do on their social media. Some people are blessed with genetics. You know the age old saying, "Black don't crack!". This statement is very true, darker skin tones age much better. If you have been blessed with a darker skin tone, you are just going to look younger longer into your older years.

However, with celebrity skincare lines, a lot more goes into looking the way they do besides just a simple skincare line that does not incorporate peptides, acids, treatments, facials and therapeutic tools. That is the main reason I wrote this book. People are always floored by my age, so I wanted to shed some light on the lifestyle you need to live, the products, serums, and tools to achieve a more youthful look.

I have personally had Botox done and I have found that a good skincare routine and using the above advanced facial modalities to be of good service for a youthful appearance. I would describe Botox as a finishing touch, and not a quick fix. Botox will not make your skin texture look amazing. Botox just stops you from being able to really express those hard lines, thus your dynamic wrinkles relax more.

There are a lot of women who get injected with many types of fillers. The past 10 years have really been a great experiment, and you can see how unnatural some of those results look on a lot of women. That is why more women are seeking out more natural ways to enhance their looks and appearance. The trick is to grow old gracefully. Let your beauty reflect wisdom, style, grace and flow. As I always say, "All women are beautiful, and beauty truly is timeless!" Our beauty flows from our core essence, it is our gift to the world.

Pro tip:

Beauty Fridge: I like putting The Naked Peach's Lemon Juice facial serum and Thirst Toner in my beauty fridge. I always wake up with a puffy face and bags under my eyes. I spritz on the cool toner and apply the Lemon Juice serum to my face. Then I use either my Jade Roller or my Micro-Current device to give myself a lymphatic drainage massage.

A lymphatic drainage massage serves to drain the buildup of lymphatic fluid within your face.

Swiping from the inner lower eye out to your ears. Swiping from your lower nostril to your lower ear. Swiping from your lower chin to lower jaw and swiping the lower jaw down the neck.

love yourself
enough to
live a
healthy
lifestyle

All You Need
Is Love
And
Skincare

64

5

Lifestyle Changes for a Youthful Look

Creating rituals in your life is the most important thing you can do to create lasting and meaningful change. If you are stressed out and living in chaos 24/7 it will take a toll on your skin's appearance and health. To age gracefully you need to learn the art of exceptional living. I read "The Art of Living" by Jim Rohn and it was a beautiful book on how to enjoy the life you have exceptionally well. If you do not have boundaries, a spiritual practice and rituals (discipline) you can never live a life worth admiring or enjoying. You have to decide which type of life are you trying to live. What is beautiful and meaningful to you? Then create a schedule that you are going to stick to, and then create this new life that brings you joy and satisfaction and helps you reach your long-term goals. The main thing of course is if you have chaos, addictions, financial lack and drama in your life; I would recommend using the system I created, which I call **STOP!** STOP is an acronym for:

1. Stabilize

2. Turn down

3. Optimize

4. Persist

If your life is not where you want it to be, you have to take time to assess where you are. STOP! Your life should not consist of running out of money, fixing and saving other people, not putting yourself first, and not taking care of yourself.

Read "Mindset" by Carol Dweck, "Co-dependent No More" by Melody Beattie and Dave Ramsey's, "The Total Money Makeover." Start reclaiming your life and stop giving your power away to others.

STOP means if your life does not function properly, then you need to STOP everything and start to stabilize before you can move forward with anything. You cannot build a house on sand. You must be standing on solid ground. Meaning, you have a stable cash flow, you can pay all of your bills on time, you have an emergency fund, your debt is manageable, you have a good credit score, you have boundaries in your relationships, you have relationships with people of integrity and character, you have encouraging and supportive relationships, and you are part of a healthy environment with like-minded individuals.

Once you have stabilized your life then you need to learn to turn down, meaning, you are not going out to eat, you are not throwing that party, you are not going on that vacation. You have to learn how to say "no" when people ask you to do things, and you are trying to save money. The answer will be, "No!" "Boundary Boss" by Terri Cole is a great book to read for anyone having issues with establishing boundaries and saying, "no."

I love this quote,

●

"Givers need to set limits because takers rarely do."

-Rachel Wolchin-

●

You have to normalize saying "no" and get used to it as part of your daily routine, so that it does not bring up anxiety or angst for you. I always say, "Stop and play the tape out" to see if your decisions lead to where you want to go. The reason why so many people live in resentment is because they say "yes" when inside they really want to say, "no." They end up over-committed and exhausted and have no time for themselves.

●

"Your boundary is only a problem for those who do not know how to respect you."

●

●

"Boundaries are basically about providing structure, and structure is essential in building anything that thrives."

●

●

"Setting boundaries is a way of caring for myself. It doesn't make me mean, selfish or uncaring just because I don't do things your way.
I care about me, too."

-Christine Morgan-

●

●

"People with no boundaries of their own have no respect for yours."

●

●

"Empathy without boundaries is Self-Destruction."

-Silvy Khoucasian-

●

●

"As empaths we are not here to be a dumping ground, a fixer, a savior or an enabler. We are here to be inspiring, attracting, activating and motivating others. People have to do their own work."

Sarah Joy-Mobley-

●

Pride is killing most people. Pride is thinking that you have all the answers, not willing to hear someone else's perspective, angling for an "ah ha" or "gotcha" moment, projecting your own issues onto someone else; so you don't have to self-reflect. Humility is the one trait that will get you everywhere and allow you to learn and grow. Anyone great in this world works with coaches, therapists, mentors and spiritual guides. You have only one life and if you think you are on an island all on your own, you are missing the ship that's sailing by to help you.

"Creative Care is Self-Care."

Sarah Joy-Mobley

Another great ritual you can add to your self-care routine is to have a creative practice, which will really help you get out of your head and into your body in the present moment; to flow. I have personally found that being creative is the most enjoyable form of self-care. I was a make-up artist for over 15 years and that was such a fulfilling career for me. I loved being able to use my craft as a creative outlet. I would easily get into flow state and then achieve an amazing look. I had to stop being a make-up artist in order to operate our salons. That was very hard because it was my main source of artistic expression for such a long time.

I had to work hard to find other ways of being creative in my business. Now, I personally block out time during my day to be creative. I call it my "9-11 Time." Yes, it's that important! It is always the most enjoyable part of my day, and the time seems to just fly by. I find that being creative is something that comes naturally to me. I can lose myself in art and other creative projects, so blocking time off for my creativity is a way to honor that need. Having a dedicated time allows me to still take care of my responsibilities and life.

There are so many ways to be creative. You just have to tap into what lights up your spirit. Some people like playing music while others like to paint. I have even seen people who enjoy cleaning, so they turn that into a creative practice. They crown themselves "The Queen of Making a Home More Beautiful." They artfully go about beautifying spaces with flowers, great aromas, interesting folds on towels, leaving candy on beds, etc. I truly believe that when you tap into what lights up your spirit and find ways to be creative in that space, is when you bring life, beauty, and art into the world. Everyone is truly creative, but some people are just blocked.

There are many ways to get creatively unblocked. You can start an art collage journal, take up jewelry design, learn how to make pottery, learn photography, take an art or creativity class. Go places where you can get inspired, where you feel more open to express yourself creatively. Make art and create something just for yourself without worrying about what others may think. You don't have to show anyone if you are just getting started. The more you practice any sort of creativity the more competent you will feel, thus building more natural confidence.

There are many studies that have been done on the benefits of having a creative practice and how it can help with reducing stress, thus making it a tremendous self-care option to add to your routine. Here is what the data shows:

1. **Reduces Stress**: Engaging in creative activities like painting, writing, or crafting significantly lowers cortisol levels (the stress hormone).

   Study: A 2016 Drexel University study found that just 45 minutes of artmaking reduced cortisol in 75% of participants.

2. **Enhances Mood**: Creative expression releases dopamine, the "feel good" neurotransmitter, which helps boost mood and motivation. People who regularly engage in creative activities report higher levels of positive emotions and life satisfaction.

3. **Improves Brain Function**: Creativity activates multiple areas of the brain, including those responsible for problem-solving, memory, and emotional regulation.

Neuroscientific research shows that creative thinking strengthens the connections between the brain's left and right hemispheres.

4. **Supports Cognitive Health**: Practices like playing music, writing, or drawing help keep the brain sharp and may reduce the risk of cognitive decline. Studies suggest that older adults who engage in creative activities experience slower memory loss and better brain health.

5. **Builds Resilience:** Creative outlets help people process trauma and adversity, making them more resilient in the face of life's challenges. Art therapy is widely used in psychological care for PTSD, anxiety, and depression.

6. **Increases Self-Awareness & Mindfulness:** Creative practices promote a state of "flow" similar to meditation, helping individuals become more present and connected with themselves. Writing in particular enhances self-reflection and can improve emotional clarity.

7. **Encourages Problem-Solving & Innovation:** Creativity trains the brain to think in non-linear ways and generate novel solutions – a skill that translates to many areas of life and work.

In short, a regular creative practice isn't just a hobby – it's a scientifically supported form of self-care that boosts your mind, mood, and overall health. Now, that is something I can get behind as a self-care option, and I can attest that throughout my life, nothing has felt better than being creative!

let food be

thy medicine

and medicine

shall be thy

food

--Hippocrates--

The mirror of your health is your skin

6

Nutritional Tips for a Youthful Feel

Often overlooked and underrated is nutrition. I learned so much about eating healthy from competing in a bodybuilding competition. I can actually look at someone and know how many calories they are eating a day and what their macro count is. To prepare for a show I had to maximize all the nutritional elements that would get me stage ready. I had to cut out everything that did not serve my goals of getting on stage. That would include no soda, no juice, no sugar, no condiments, no bread, and no pasta. Everything had to be measured and weighed to achieve optimal results.

The bodybuilding diet consists of high protein, and low carbs and fats that would be considered in the Mediterranean diet profile.

If you want a nice body you will never get it by only working out. We all know those people who work out for years and nothing ever changes. Abs are made in the kitchen. If you want a toned and muscular physique that you can be proud of then you need to work on eating healthy foods. There are Four Pillars to maintaining a healthy diet:

❖ Total calorie input

❖ Protein

❖ Carbs

❖ Fats

A good gauge that I go by when talking to people is that it is healthy to lose two pounds a week. To figure out your macro content for the day, what you should be eating to either maintain, lose or gain muscle. You can go to:-
www.calculator.net/macro-calculator.html and input your age, weight, height, goals etc. They will give you a macro count to follow.

Example: I am 5' 10" tall, and 144 pounds. I work out five-six days a week. I would like to maintain my current frame. This is what my goal looks like:

❖ Protein: 158 grams per day (634 calories)

❖ Carbs: 211 grams per day (845 calories)

❖ Fats: 70 grams per day (634 calories)

❖ Total calories: 2113

The next thing you want to do is meal-prep your food so you can hit your nutritional goals every day. I meal-prep on Sunday. Check out the hashtag #mealprepsunday online. You can purchase meal-prep bags to carry with you every day. My favorite one is from 6 Pack Fitness. Their name always reminds me that abs are made in the kitchen! You can purchase their bags online or at GNC.

You can also purchase a food measuring scale from the grocery store or on amazon.com. Everyone always jokes in the bodybuilding community that the only ones who ever use those scales are bodybuilders and drug dealers.

The scale works great because it allows you to measure your food in grams and ounces. I usually prep oatmeal, brown rice, quinoa or sweet potato as my healthy carb source. Then I prep fish or Beyond Meat Vegan meat, and spinach or broccoli. I will typically use olive oil, avocado or peanut butter as my healthy fat source. I also use Owyn Vegan Protein Shakes two- three times a day to fill in the protein gap. They contain 35 grams of protein per shake.

You want to make sure you are eating every two-three hours to make sure you are hitting your macro intake of calories throughout the day. You will find that you have sustained energy all day and don't have to do the normal Red Bull and coffee rush throughout the day.

I do love a good cup of coffee! I use Stevia in my coffee as a substitute for sugar. I also will put protein powder in my coffee to make myself feel like I'm having some creamer.

Drinking water throughout the day is essential. You should drink at least half a gallon or more of water. Water helps rid the body of toxins and waste, keeps you hydrated and helps to get rid of cellulite.

If you want to train for a competition I always suggest working with a personal trainer who is experienced in prepping people for shows. A Carb Cycle Diet is what you will have to be on. You should follow the above protocol, however you would be cycling your carbs and fats to low ratios, so you need a professional to guide you; to help and keep a watchful eye over your progress. I do not suggest carb cycling on your own as it can be dangerous if you do not know what you're doing.

Supplements are a great addition to any nutritional regime. I personally like to take a multi-vitamin, vitamin C, B-complex, calcium, vitamin D, zinc and iron. Upon researching the topic of longevity and listening to some podcasts by Dr. David Sinclair PhD, a Harvard professor, I just added into my regime the anti-aging supplements he suggested in his talks. I took a semi deep dive into the data backing up his claims and have become a believer in taking Berberine, NMN and Resveratrol supplements.

In my research I was able to find out that the World Health Organization, which released the 11th Edition of its International Classification of Diseases, added that for the first time aging is a disease. Scientists at Harvard have discovered how to reverse the aging process through their trials with mice. This has opened up a whole new discussion as to aging being something we do not have to partake in, if we make self-care choices that prolong life. Having a healthy self-care practice is a major factor in longevity and health. Managing the domains of stress, foods/supplements, exercise and skincare; you can expect to have many more years of health and a great quality of life.

Scientists have found out that there are certain foods, supplements, exercise and choices you can partake in to prolong your life by 10 plus years. This science is only getting started. Dr. David Sinclair, PhD has written extensively on this topic in his book titled, "Lifespan."

Harvard scientists have discovered that NAD (nicotinamide adenine dinucleotide), a co-enzyme present in all living cells, and present across all species of life; triggers shifts that enhance survival, boosts energy production and regulates cellular repair.

By middle age our NAD levels will plummet to half of that in our youth. Numerous studies have shown that boosting NAD levels increases insulin sensitivity, reverses mitochondrial dysfunction and extends lifespan.

Taken orally, NAD suppresses age related adipose tissue inflammation, enhances insulin action, improves mitochondrial function and neuronal function in the brain. These benefits help with diabetes and Alzheimer's.

Berberine is another supplement you can take that has great potential to regulate glucose and lipid homeostasis, cancer growth and inflammation. Berberine is a supplement that works similar to the prescription Metformin. Metformin is a drug that people take for diabetes. Metformin, which is derived from French lilac, has been shown to help with slowing aging and increasing lifespan. Metformin is a drug you have to get a prescription for. Berberine has been shown to provide the same benefits as Metformin in supplement form.

Resveratrol is another supplement you can take that helps your body fight cancer and heart disease. Resveratrol acts like an antioxidant protecting your body. Resveratrol is contained in red grapes, peanuts, and red wine. There is a lot of data from the National Library of Medicine stating that Resveratrol can help with anti-aging and longevity through increasing DNA repair capacities.

What's really exciting is that scientists are now able to determine someones biological age verses their chronological age. While chronological age refers to the actual amount of time a person has been living, biological age is determined by the way your body has changed over time. This is determined by how fast our cells are deteriorating, our genes, our lifestyle and exercise habits. We have all seen those individuals who have poor health habits and look much older than they are, and some people who seem to look very young for their chronological age. There even have been arguments that some people can and should be able to change their age to fit their biological age; so that they do not face ageism.

Ageism is similar to sexism and racism, in which the person is being discriminated against because of their chronological age. A person who has been biologically healthy their whole lives can face ageism for work opportunities, procreating older and marrying younger individuals. There are many individuals who

80

have a very young biological clock and are discriminated against for their chronological age. These new discoveries are very exciting because they show evidence that people can live 10-30 years longer than normally expected, based on studies done by Harvard scientists and Dr. David Sinclair.

To find out your biological age go to: www.tallyhealth.com, they will have a mouth swab test coming out soon.

*Always consult with your doctor before beginning any dietary, exercise or supplement change.

to keep the body
in good health is
a duty otherwise
we shall not be
able to keep our
mind strong and
clear

--Buddha--

Sarah Joy-Mobley, Miami Florida

7

Workout Tips for Youthfulness

Working out is the single most important thing that you can do to increase your youthfulness, vibrancy, strength, tone and overall attractiveness. As human beings we are attracted to strength and health. Having a beautifully toned, tight, muscular and fit body is a sign of health and fitness. There is a reason why men go to the gym to enhance their physiques. Simply put, it's evolution. Studies have shown that women prefer stronger looking men. A study done of 170 women in Australia found that women prefer men based on three main points: how strong he is, how lean he is, and how tall he is.

Studies have shown that being fit is consistently the highest rated factor for attractiveness in both men and women. Recent studies show that fit women are more attractive than thin women. Psychologically, confident people are more magnetic. Physically strong people are more confident in their prowess and ability to defend themselves physically. A sign of being an Alpha female or Alpha male is dominance in strength. Working out releases endorphins and feelings of euphoria that lead to a greater sense of well-being.

Based on human evolution, both sexes are attracted to fitness because we are biologically signaled this way. A fit body signals to both sexes the ability to survive a famine, survive a fatal disease, and the ability to care for other tribe members and offspring.

There is never an excuse not to workout. We only have so much willpower in any given day. I always say force yourself to work out first thing in the morning, as the day drags on it is hard to find the motivation and willpower. Willpower is a muscle that has to be worked over time to build up. You have to use your willpower to get started with a new habit and then allow that habit to carry you over time.

The advent of the internet and social media has made it clear that there is never a time when you can't work out. I love telling people to go on a walk every day for a half hour or do a HIIT (high interval intensity training) workout. HIIT gives you the most bang for your buck working out. A HIIT workout involves short bursts of intense training followed by low- intensity training. Studies have shown that this style of workout can equal an hour of normal style training, and you get great results. You can burn a lot of calories in a short amount of time as well. HIIT increases your metabolism more than regular exercise. HIIT is a great way to gain muscle and lose fat. Think about how the body of a sprinter looks verses a marathon runner, to get an idea of the effects of a HIIT workout. The sprinter is doing high intensity body functions, and the marathon runner is doing a fitness style that will not necessarily build muscle.

Here is an example of a HIIT training routine that you can do on your own (keep the intensity high for five minutes and low for five minutes, repeat):

1. **Ten minutes: jumping jacks**

2. **Ten minutes: squats**

3. **Ten minutes: sprints**

4. **Ten minutes: sit ups**

You can also go online and watch videos on how to create your own workout. Ultimately, if you really want to take your health seriously you should hire a personal trainer. There are many people who spend money on clubbing, restaurants, shows, concerts and at bars. Yet, when it comes to their health they won't spend a dime. Just do a simple experiment. Track how much money you spend on entertainment, going out, having fun, etc. for the month. Now take half of that money and put it towards a gym membership, a personal trainer and eating healthy foods.

I like for people to work out with a trainer if they are a newbie to the health and wellness scene. That way they can properly learn the basics to gain muscle and lose fat. Once they have a base knowledge than they can go off and do their own thing. However, many people need someone to hold them accountable to work out and that's their purpose for hiring a trainer.

Another great way to work out is with a group of people. This has been coined "bootcamp." Doing group bootcamps is a great way to get personal training without the cost of one-on-one training. There are a lot of companies and trainers who offer this service. However, no matter who you are, you should be getting at least 30-60 minutes a day of exercise. This can be walking, taking the stairs, jogging or jumping jacks. On rainy days walk up and down the stairs in your house for 30 minutes. You truly have no excuse. It helps with your mental, physical and spiritual health on so many levels!

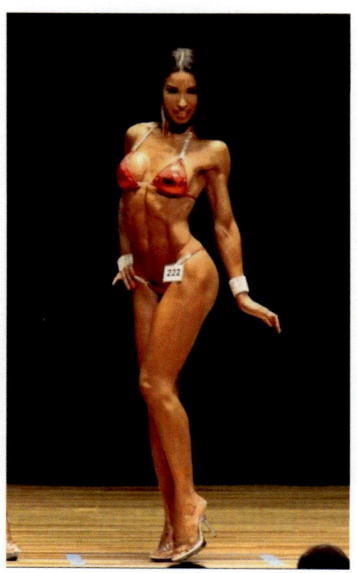

April 19th, 2014 Placed 1st Place Women's Masters Bikini John Kemper Classic

Questions & Answers

Why is it important to support local small businesses?

Can you imagine a neighborhood or city without all of its local small businesses? It would be a ghost town something out of an apocalypse movie.

The Small Business Administration (SBA) reports that there are 28 million small businesses operating in the US. Those small businesses generate 66% of all new jobs in the United States.

Small businesses support your town by paying sales tax, city and county taxes where the business is located. Those taxes support the schools, parks, roads, sidewalks, and fund public service workers like firefighters. When you stray to big box retailers that money doesn't benefit the local community.

According to civic economics, on average 48% of each purchase at local independent businesses is recirculated locally, compared to less than 14% of purchases at chain stores.

Small businesses according to the SBA have created more than half the jobs in the US. According to the SBA, big businesses have eliminated more than 4,000,000 jobs, while small businesses have added more than 8,000,000 jobs.

Small businesses typically provide better customer service because their survival depends on being more personable and hands on.

Small businesses create a sense of community. You are more likely to meet the owner of a small business than the CEO of a Fortune 500 Company. Get involved and shop small, knowing that you are supporting your local economy.

At The Naked Peach we have donated over $47,000 in scholarships to Philadelphians in need and to local charities. We donated $5,000 to Philabundance towards their initiative to "End Hunger for Good." This program is something that we can get behind as a salon, because the program gives the students the skill sets to survive. The program promotes self- sufficiency by preparing the students to work in the food industry. The program lasts 16 weeks for a total of 500 hours. The students will also learn critical life skills for future success.

Why do you use hard wax at The Naked Peach Salons?

As a licensed Esthetician Teacher and licensed Advanced Esthetician it is very important for me to use best practices from The Milady Esthetician Standard Textbook. The Milady book is written by industry professionals who have consulted with educators, doctors, state officials and nurses on what the best protocols should be and the safest procedures to use.

On page 488 of the Milady Standard Esthetician book required for state board exams, they state that **hard wax "is the wax to use for coarse hair** and soft wax for larger body areas."

I have been in the industry for 25 years and have an opportunity to use all kinds of waxes. I have also come to the conclusion that hard wax is the best wax for that area. Unlike any other area of the body, the skin there is more sensitive, with different types of skin folds to manage, plus the hair is coarse and grows in many different directions.

In order to properly and effectively wax people's lady parts it is important to use a wax that is the safest and most effective.

Hard wax adheres to the hair and not the skin. Hard wax shrink wraps around the coarse hairs of the Brazilian area and can be removed in any way. Hard wax does not require muslin strips be pulled off. Hard wax dries to a hardened consistency, after which it can be removed on its own.

At The Naked Peach we have our hard wax custom made so that we can maintain the quality of the ingredients in the wax.

The Naked Peach's wax is made with:

1. Beeswax, which is a natural humectant filled with protective wax esthers.

2. Paraffin, which is a natural emollient helping the skin to stay soft and supple.

3. Natural oils, which moisturizes the skin and helps reduce inflammation.

At The Naked Peach we use The 15-Minute Comfort Hard Wax Technique!

1. Cleanse the skin with Calm Down Toner (cucumber toner)

2. Powder the skin with corn starch (to protect the skin)

3. Use holds and pressure for comfort

4. Apply Relax Oil (sweet almond oil) to soothe post wax

5. Reapply Calm Down Toner to cool the skin post wax

We also never double dip with our sticks! A new stick is used every time we put it in the pot, then we throw the stick in the trash. Alcohol is sprayed down after every client and all tweezers are kept in Barbacide.

We also get you in and out in 15 minutes. An experienced Esthetician will be able to get a Brazilian wax done in less than 20 minutes. The shorter the wax time, the greater the experience of the esthetician when it comes to Brazilian waxing. Plus, no one wants to keep their legs spread eagle for more than 15 minutes! Your legs start cramping!

Are the skincare products at The Naked Peach vegan?

Yes, all of the skincare items are vegan, paraben free, animal cruelty free and made in the USA. The Naked Peach Skincare line has been curated by Sarah Joy-Mobley. The products are all made with highly concentrated, high quality botanical extracts, natural moisturizers, natural exfoliants, vitamin C derivatives, natural oils, marine extracts and effective vitamins that drive results.

You can go to our website www.thenakedpeach.com to find out more about our product ingredients and details.

Our custom made wax is made outside of the United States.

What are Sarah Joy-Mobley's qualifications, the owner of The Naked Peach?

Sarah is a licensed Esthetician Teacher (500 hours), licensed Esthetician (300 hours), and licensed Advanced Esthetician (70 hours). She also holds an AA degree from The University of Arizona in Business, and a PhD in Organizational Leadership from IMHS.

She has 25 years of experience working in the esthetics industry as a make-up artist, technician and instructor. She has 12 years of experience as a salon operator.

How long have The Naked Peach Salons been in Philadelphia?

The Naked Peach Salons have been in Philadelphia for 12 years. We started our first salon on South Street then expanded to Roxborough, Queens Village, and we are now in Haverford. Our training center and Corporate offices are in Montgomeryville, PA.

Has Sarah Joy-Mobley worked with celebrities?

Yes, prior to opening the salon. Sarah worked with numerous celebrity clients doing their make-up and at make-up events for Sean Combs, Marcia Ambrosia, Christina Milian, Jersey Shore's J WOWW, Perez Hilton and others.

Why did you stop working as a make-up artist?

I always dreamed of owning a business. I never saw myself as talent. I always saw myself as the one writing the checks to the talent. I have always been interested in who the manager, leader or owner of a company was. I always watched people lead and the environment they created and how it felt, looked and the experience they were able to create, especially if there was a women in charge. I always noticed that when the ladies led, they seemed to care more about the little things and took more of a personal interest in others. The environment felt more nurturing and caring if that makes sense. I always felt safer when the ladies were in charge and had the money to make decisions. Women tend to learn humility quickly and are more diplomatic when conflicts occur. Women will not burn down the farm to prove a point. We got kids to feed!

My whole life I had to lead myself because I was always on my own at crucial and critical stages of my growth. I always noticed poor leadership, so watching who led well was important to me. I remember so many times my life going into chaos, because of poor leadership. I just knew that if I had a chance to lead. I would make sure to create an environment that would be sustainable. The bills are paid, lights are on, we always make payroll, we make wise decisions, we seek wisdom and knowledge, we stay humble and are eager to learn.

I always had a fighting spirit and became strong through adversity, and I find those are the very things you really need to be a leader.

Can you give advice to people wanting to become an esthetician?

Yes, I always recommend finding a school that fits your comfort level. Schools will teach you the basics to pass state board exams. However, it is up to you to take advanced classes and advanced services when you are out of school. I always recommend specializing in one service. Also, it takes about 10 years to become a master of a craft, like eyelashes, acrylic nails, Brazilian waxer, make-up and facial knowledge. They say it takes 10,000 hours to become an expert at something. Specialize in one thing and become the best at that. That gives you a sense of pride, knowing that you are one of the best in your field.

Do you plan on franchising The Naked Peach?

I have had many offers, and we have had to protect our Trademark many times. I have to respect the journey and the process of my growth as a leader, and I take the steps according to what feels right for our salons' health and welfare in the current economic state of the country. I study the economy. I consult with experts in business and make decisions accordingly.

I never make a decision based on money alone or how something will look to others. I make a decision based on, does it feel right, is it right, will it benefit my whole team, is it sustainable, does it make financial sense, can I keep my sanity, does it fit into my value system and lifestyle goals?

I have learned as a leader that you have to say "no" to a lot of things. Just because it's hot or trending doesn't mean it is sustainable long-term or a good business model to follow.

I am never looking to chase money, chase attention, or looking to hop on trends. I am interested in building a sustainable business that supports my team and our community.

Currently, we have no plans to franchise. However, we are currently entering business partnerships with trusted long-- term team members.

Do you plan on opening more Naked Peaches?

Right now we have put things on hold because of the economy. The current state of affairs in America has made it hard to make intelligent financial decisions with inflation running hot, war going on and supply chain shortages.

However, if the right opportunity comes along and it makes sustainable long-term sense for the salons and our current team; then we could possibly take advantage of another salon.

The current business plan is to take it one day at a time, until we have more stability in the economy. Update! We've now opened another salon in Haverford, PA!

What did you do during the pandemic shutdown?

The pandemic shutdown was a time of confusion and chaos for everyone. There were a lot of business owners who were looking around for help, in shock, going out of business or falling apart.

The one thing I am good at is functioning in a time of crisis. I actually felt that during the pandemic it was finally a chance for me to shine as a leader.

I would consider myself an adversity leader. An adversity leader is someone who has had to survive in the world on their own and overcome obstacles. A peace-time leader is someone who learned and was mentored by others without risks or adversity.

During the pandemic my senses were heightened like being in a street fight. Everything was crystal clear, and my intuition was operating at full capacity. You have to trust your instincts in times of crisis.

The only way your intuition functions is if you have a code of ethics you abide by and you don't lie to yourself. You have to become a seeker of truth and be willing to change your beliefs based on new information. Then your intuition is your North Star in life, your GPS and your compass. Then you will be able to trust yourself and your decision making.

I have always followed a value system at the salons. I do not chase money, trends or hop on a money grab. I am only interested in building a long-term sustainable business that can grow in a consistent-sustainable way; one that benefits everyone who works together as a team.

I watch the economy closely by following many different economists online. I follow people who are generally first principal thinkers and well-educated.

I was well aware that we were headed into a financial disaster right before the pandemic. I had been saving and making sure the salons could ride out a financial storm. However, I did not expect there to be a pandemic shutdown.

I had been saving and stockpiling supplies at our warehouse, when the pandemic hit. I was able to pay my staff for two weeks out of my own pocket. Then they were all easily able to get on unemployment.

The only employee that was still working full time was our warehouse manager. He was able to assist in sending packages from online orders to our clients, so they could keep up their skincare routines at home.

During the shutdown. I made available care packages to our employees. I was able to send them paper towels, baby wipes and skincare products. I was also able to provide loans to the employees who needed them.

I tried my best to keep everyone's spirits high while we all waited around to see when we could reopen.

Then the government started to give out PPP loans to businesses that were struggling. I have studied the economy long enough to know that as a business owner, it's up to you to manage your affairs in such a way that you can be resilient and have a strong balance sheet.

I always had on my mind to be a good Girl Scout, even though I was never in the Girl Scouts. I would recommend sending your girls to Girl Scouts to learn leadership skills, it will serve them well in life.

I also was well aware of the effects and hazards of giving people free money, because of the fact that I used to be homeless and on welfare as a teenager. I was well aware of the crippling effects of giving people something they did not earn on their own; and the crippling effect it has on your ability to trust yourself to be able to be strong, resilient and self- sufficient. You and you alone can figure things out and take measurable actions to advance in a problem-solving way.

I knew it was going to be tough to get the salons back up and running. However, I was going to stick to my principles. I was not going to take a handout. Come hell or hot water, we were going to navigate this as a team and recover.

During the pandemic we also stopped all membership payments and billed no one during those three months. I was well aware of the major franchise chains who charged their members during that time. However, I knew people were struggling so I went with my gut and did what I felt was the right thing to do and put everyone's memberships on hold.

I had to pay a software engineer to remote into our computers for several weeks, in order to reprogram our software to stop those payments.

We faced a lot of difficulties with trying to run the salons with constant overnight mandates and mask wearing policies. Also, we were limited to the services that we could do. The biggest challenge was just managing peoples' fear responses. Some people have an enormous fear response, and others have a more robust nervous system. I have learned to be diplomatic and respect everyone's decisions and choices. That is the beauty of living in America. We have choice, freedom of speech and dominion over our own bodies. However, we managed and were able to get back on our feet.

I am so grateful to the core of my staff that believed in my leadership and stuck with me through those challenges! My heart was so overwhelmed when one of my employees sent me a card telling me how much she admired my leadership during the pandemic.

My heart just gets so overwhelmed with gratitude to know that my staff is with me and I am fighting so hard so that we all can win together!

When I say win, that means staying open as a brick and mortar business. We have been hitting payroll for 12 years straight. Paying all of our city taxes and payroll taxes, as well as giving to charity. That is quite a huge task. The statistics are that 18.4% of businesses fail in first year, 49.7% fail in five years, and 65.5% fail in 10 years.

The reason being is that running a business is hard. You have to have a rock-solid resolution, strong character and be tough as nails. People will challenge you, steal from you, slander you. Success brings contempt.

Do you have a favorite salon?

I love all the salons equally. I feel like each salon has its own charm, flavor and vibe. What's really exciting is that the girls who work at the salons decorate for all the holidays, which keeps things festive for everyone.

I always want everyone who walks into the salons to feel cared for, valued and to receive great service!

Our current staff does an amazing job delivering that Vision!

Do I have to stick with one technician at The Naked Peach?

Our salons are set up where everyone is learning the same Naked Peach protocols. We have some technicians who have worked in the industry longer than others. However, I always recommend getting to know a few waxers, so that if your current tech is out on vacation or sick you have an alternative to go to!

I always suggest that it is best to stick to your waxing schedule of waxing every four to six weeks for the best results.

What is the most common question asked during a Brazilian wax that is really comical?

It's funny but a lot of women ask how their lady parts compare to other women's lady parts. I always have to chuckle when someone asks me. Honestly they all look the same to me. All women have exactly the same equipment.

When I'm doing a Brazilian wax it's like waxing any other body part. You get used to waxing lady parts and it's just like doing someone's nails.

All of us women have the same parts, so you never have to feel uncomfortable getting a wax. Waxing for us is just another day at The Naked Peach.

At our salon everyone is welcome regardless of their age, sex, weight, height, style, image, religion, beliefs, color of skin, or disability. The only thing we require is respect, treating people with dignity and kindness.

What was your most memorable Brazilian wax?

I was waxing a regular client who was a long time member with us. She was always so nice and personable every time she came into the salon. Her tech happened to be out that week. So, I was more than happy to accommodate her.

I let her get undressed in the room as I waited outside of the door until she was finished undressing . I knocked on the door to see if she was ready.

Upon entering the room nothing seemed to be out of the ordinary, so I proceeded to go about my business of getting her brazilian wax done efficiently and quickly.

Lord knows no woman likes to sit spread eagle for too long. Their legs start to hurt, they get a Charliehorse cramp, and their legs start shaking!

Anyway, I start waxing underneath her bottom area first as I always do. Start from the bottom and work our way up. It's a little industry trick we do. To do the least painful first , so by the time you get to the more "Ew wee!" parts you are done! Like magic!

Once I put her legs down to wax the top part of her Brazilian area. I noticed that she had what looked like whip marks all along her legs. Upon further inspection it looked like it was a barb wire mark! I'm sitting over here in my head like, "Hold on a minute here! Is this women getting abused?" Being the humanitarian I am. I had to speak up and say something because I was worried about her safety.

I asked her if she was in an abusive relationship and if she needed any help. Well, come to find out, she goes on to tell me that she is into S&M. I mean the 50 Shades of Grey S&M, like there is a whole community out there that's into this stuff. They sign contracts with each other to say what they can and cannot do to each other during their rendezvous. Well, talk about, "Spilling the Tea!" I was like a fly on the wall! What?

Well, anyway she would come see me over the next few months, and her stories would get more wild and raunchy every time. I said, "Lord have mercy, you crazy girl!". I couldn't stop listening to these stories 'cause they seemed straight from a movie or a book!

I will tell you she was my most memorable client and quite a great storyteller!

What do you suggest for getting rid of ingrown hairs?

The best way to get rid of ingrown hairs is to keep up with your after care. When you are being waxed, hair is pulled out from the root. This hair will grow back slowly over the next four to eight weeks. It is important to keep your hair follicles clear of any dead skin and free of bacteria.

Bumps be Done and Rehab Me are our two aftercare products that are our best sellers. For good reason! They work! We even have men from barber shops come in to purchase the Bumps be Done. We even have clients who move out of state and still order our products online.

The biggest reason I see people getting ingrown hairs is that they are not using their after-care products correctly. When in the shower use Rehab Me scrub for a full 30-60 seconds and scrub vigorously. Actually, time yourself while you do it. Most people scrub for five seconds. Scrubbing for the full 30-60 seconds really makes sure your pores are clear, and the hair will come out clean. Also, apply a pea-size amount of the Bumps be Done two or three days a week as well for maximum effectiveness. If you have any ingrown hairs they will easily pop out in the shower.

Also, some people are just not waxing candidates. Just like everyone can't eat peanuts. But that doesn't mean the whole world has to stop eating peanuts because some people are allergic. The same thing applies to waxing.

Bumps be Done and Rehab Me work by using AHA and BHA acids. These acids work by exfoliating the skin and BHA works to unclog the follicles, specifically salicylic acid.

I'm sensitive, so how can I make the Brazilian wax hurt less?

The best way to make sure the Brazilian Wax does not hurt as much is to make sure you do not wax within four days of your menstrual cycle or you will be more sensitive. Take a Tylenol or Advil an hour before your wax. Make sure not to drink coffee or alcohol within 12 hours of your wax. Alcohol and caffeine will make you more sensitive during a wax.

You also can come into the salon a half-hour prior to your appointment and for an extra $5 to get some numbing creme.

However, I will say we do a good job keeping it as pain free as possible. By using hard wax, using skin holds, pressure, as well as breathing techniques.

What is the difference between intrinsic aging and extrinsic aging?

Intrinsic aging is what the Good Lord blessed you with. That would be your genetics, hereditary factors, skin color and your actual chronological age.

Extrinsic aging is all the exposure you have had to the elements and environment over the lifetime of your skin. Specially smoking, sun, pollutants and poor health habits. These are the things that you can avoid!

What are the worst things that you can do to damage your skin?

1. Sun exposure
2. Smoking
3. Excessive alcohol
4. Using drugs
5. Picking at your skin
6. Not using sunblock
7. Poor health habits
8. Not utilizing proper skincare
9. Poor sleeping habits

What is the scope of practice of an esthetician?

Estheticians are skincare specialists. They are knowledgeable in how to beautify your skin. They can recommend skincare products for you. They can help unclog and clean out your pores. They can do skin care treatments, facial treatments, facial massage, make-up, body treatments, spray tanning, eyelash extensions, eyebrow and lash treatments, advanced facial treatments (some states require an Advanced Esthetic License).

What can estheticians not do?

Hair, nails, full body massage, tattoo of the face or body, laser (some states are different), injections, prescribe medicine or give medical advice.

What is an Esthetician Teacher?

An esthetician who has acquired more hours than a normal esthetician to continue their education in the field of Esthetics; and is licensed to train and certify hours for other estheticians so they can pass their state board exam at a Cosmetology School or Esthetician School (some states allow apprenticeships).

What is it like to be an esthetician?

Being an esthetician is really fun. You get to show up every day for work ready to beautify someone. They are going to be really happy that you made them look and feel beautiful! You are not saddled with a ton of student debt from being in college for four years. You can be in and out of school in less than a year. You start working quickly in your field and be self-sufficient and ready to start an amazing life that is sustainable! If you take your career seriously you can make more money than people with college degrees!

How do you feel about industry shade?

I don't judge anyone anymore because I don't want anyone judging me. There are many people in the world who are living in desperate situations, they are barely surviving, they are living hand-to-mouth, and in poverty. There are so many people who lack even the basic necessities for survival and lack any type of advanced education. Lord only knows the struggles in people's hearts and pain they are going through like traumas and unaddressed disadvantages.

I can only have this understanding and compassion because I am someone who has had a disadvantaged past as well. I am very much aware that when someone is throwing shade at me it is because they are hurting inside themselves. Even worse, they might have had every blessing in life and never been challenged, so they have no strength. Their lives are filled with fear, jealousy and resentment. I also have compassion for that. Living in a constant state of fear is a terrible place to be. I am empathic to that. Content people lift others up, they build, they support and they create. Underdeveloped people attack, slander and tear down.

The ultimate truth is we all have to do our own work. When we are jealous of others we just need to listen to our own hearts and start working on ourselves. No one is coming to save us or save the day. We all have to put our big-girl panties on and build the lives we want for ourselves. Until you can take 100%

responsibility for your own life and stop blaming others you will always live in distress; and find someone to attack, projecting your unaddressed insecurities on them.

How have you been able to be successful as an esthetician?

I always try and give 100%, every time I provide a service. I always go above and beyond to make sure the client is happy. If I am not sure about something I will always try and find the right solution and information needed. I also take pride in doing a job well done. I personally love it when I can lift someone's spirits and make them feel better, even if it's just for a moment.

I have found that I've learned how to become a therapist, a comedian, a counselor and a friend to so many. I am sure I have helped people in so many ways that I am not even aware of. I do believe that is why the Lord keeps my life blessed.

I always felt so fulfilled and happy being a technician because people give you instant love and validation. It's like a love fest!

When I started to become overwhelmed with running the salons and being a technician. I had to make the choice to step away from being a technician. Now, mind you that I spent my whole life's work being a make-up artist and a technician. I was the best at what I did and had plenty of confidence.

I had no idea of the enormous task it would be to run a salon. I would say that running the salons has shaped my character and made me a better person. I have strong fortitude and a strong value system because of it, and I learned to set boundaries.

I had to learn the new skill set of leading and not being the talent. I made a commitment and come hell or high water I had to figure it out.

I find that with leadership there is no figuring it out in advance. You are always evolving and figuring things out as you go. When you lead, the landscape is always changing. Who would have thought that we would close down the world for three months during the pandemic?

I know so many business owners who lost their businesses or could not function with the mandates.

I will say thank goodness we are a Brazilian waxing shop. That is the main reason we were able to open right back up! We did away with the facials because it was too hard to stay safe without masks etc.

By the grace of God, prayer is always part of our business plan.

Now that I am a business owner and have fully stepped into this position, I am trying to be the best business owner and leader possible. This year's Goals are to attract a DREAM TEAM and DREAM CLIENTS and also create leading ladies!

You've got to get in, where you fit in; where you and your clients like the environment and how things are done. If our staff likes our environment and how we do things, we all thrive. Please come on down and stay a while if you like. I'm okay with not having to be everything to everyone!

That is where my faith comes in. What I have learned in life is that what God has meant for you, nobody can tear down or destroy. This is your blessing, your mission and your purpose.

What are the core values of The Naked Peach?

We believe in diversity, giving back, self-care and leadership for women. We hire a diverse staff from all different backgrounds, races, ages, sexual orientation, religions and beliefs. We believe that by coming together we are more alike than different. Women happen to make great leaders. I find that if a women can successfully manage a household then she is perfectly capable of a management and leadership position. We also pledge $5,000 a year to charity. The charities that we currently support are Philabundance and <u>TreePhilly.org</u>. Total giving to date is $47,000 to local charities and vocational scholarships. We feel that the best way to meaningfully support our environment is to help plant more trees. This directly and practically helps improve the environmental issues we face locally.

I have faith in humanity. That faith is in the willingness of entrepreneurs to respond and create solutions to many of life's pressing issues. That faith is very optimistic.

You can purchase a Self-Love Journal at our salons. You may also go online to make a purchase as well.

Self-Love Affirmations

I accept myself just the way I am, flaws and all. I am made in the image and likeness of God. I am loved unconditionally by my higher power. I am his finest creation. I am supported by the Universe. I am unique, just like a snow flake or a fingerprint. There is no one else like me. I am one-of-a-kind. I am blessed and highly favored. I have gifts within me that need to be shared with the world. I am a gem. I am kind to myself. I am my own best friend. I put myself and my own needs first. I take care of myself every day and give myself what I need to feel good and sustain my own sense of joy. I love myself.

Gratitude Affirmations

Thank you. I have everything I need. I am a good steward of everything I have in my life. I am faithful over my home, car, career, business, purpose, mind, body, spirit, family, friends and belongings. I am blessed beyond measure. I have everything I need to take the next step in every area of my life. My heart is filled with peace, faith, hope and thankfulness. I am attracting all the right people, knowledge, wisdom and circumstances into my life. I am so blessed, so filled with gratitude that my cup spills over into others' lives. I am a person of value. I am a giver. I am open and ready for excellence and abundance in all areas of my life. I am ready to step into my greatness.

How to get in touch with us!

Shop for products at: **www.thenakedpeach.com**

Come visit our salons in Philadelphia:

How to get in touch with Sarah!

Website:

http://www.thenakedpeach.com

Email:

peachysarahjoy@gmail.com

Find Sarah on Social Media!

@drsarahjoymobley on LinkedIn

Mail:

P.O. Box 721

Sellersville, PA 18960

Sarah Joy-Mobley, Self Care Advocate

Sarah Joy-Mobley is the founder of The Naked Peach Salons in Philadelphia. She is a Licensed Esthetician, Licensed Advanced Esthetician and Licensed Esthetician Teacher. She has an AA in Business from The University of Arizona, and a PhD in Organizational Leadership from IMHS. She has a rich history of being in the Esthetics Industry for over 25 years as a make-up artist, esthetician and instructor.

Her salons have been in Philadelphia for 12 years. She has 24 people on full time payroll. She pays the highest commissions to employees in her industry. Her motto is, "As a team we succeed together!."

She has competed and won 1st place Masters Bikini A in the premier fitness organization NPC (National Physique Committee) Bev Francis Show in New Jersey 2014.

She is passionate about health and wellness and strives to share her knowledge about the benefits of Self Care and longevity. She is a Self Care Advocate and encourages everyone to start taking better care of themselves! You above anyone else deserve your Love first!

Closing Prayer

I just wanted to end this book with knowing that I touched someones heart. I know life can seem hard at times. It is so important to keep the faith and be strong. Just keep on moving and keep listening to your heart. You have a song inside of you that you need to sing to the world. That song is just for you to sing. Don't let no body make you feel any less than or that you are not worth something! You are worth something. You have worth, you have rarity and we are all made in the image and likeliness of something great and supreme! We are all equals on a spiritual level.

May many blessings of prosperity flourish over your life. May your life become rivers of choice, deliverance, peace, joy, and blessings of many kinds.

a man's belly shall be satisfied with the fruit of his mouth and with the increase of his lips shall he be filled death and life are in the power of the tongue and they that love it will eat the fruit thereof

--Proverbs 18:21--

finally brothers and sisters whatever is true whatever is noble whatever is right whatever is pure whatever is lovely whatever is admirable if anything is excellent or praiseworthy think of such things

--Philippians 4:8--